Killer Staffing Skills Managers Need To Know

Tips And Techniques That Managers Can Use In Order To Develop Leadership Skills

"Practical, proven techniques that will help you to manage your Manager career successfully"

Dr. Jim Anderson

Published by:
Blue Elephant Consulting
Tampa, Florida

Copyright © 2019 by Dr. Jim Anderson

All rights reserved. No part of this book may be reproduced of transmitted in any form or by any means, electronic or mechanical, including photocopying, recording or by any information storage and retrieval system without written permission of the publisher, except for inclusion of brief quotations in a review.

Printed in the United States of America

Library of Congress Control Number: 2018913471

ISBN-13: 9781795044264

Warning – Disclaimer

The purpose of this book is to educate and entertain. This book does not promise or guarantee that anyone following the ideas, tips, suggestions, techniques or strategies will be successful. The author, publisher and distributor(s) shall have neither liability nor responsibility to anyone with respect to any loss or damage caused, or alleged to be caused, directly or indirectly by the information contained in this book.

Recent Books By The Author

Product Management

- Developing World Class Products: Techniques For Product Managers To Better Understand What Their Customers Really Want

- Managing Your Product Manager Career: How Product Managers Can Find And Succeed In The Right Job

Public Speaking

- Unforgettable Presentations That Can Change The World: Presentation techniques that will transform a speech into a memorable event

- Creating Speeches That Work: How To Create A Speech That Will Make Your Message Be Remembered Forever!

CIO Skills

- Communication Skills That Every CIO Must Have: Tips And Techniques For CIOs To Use In Order To Become Better Communicators

- How CIOs Can Bring Business And IT Together: How CIOs Can Use Their Technical Skills To Help Their

Company Solve Real-World Business Problems

IT Manager Skills

- How IT Managers Can Use New Technology To Meet Today's IT Challenges: Technologies That IT Managers Can Use In Order to Make Their Teams More Productive

- How To Build High Performance IT Teams: Tips And Techniques That IT Managers Can Use In Order To Develop Productive Teams

Negotiating

- The Art Of Packaging A Negotiation: How To Develop The Skill Of Assembling Potential Trades In Order To Get The Best Possible Outcome

- Getting What You Want In A Negotiation By Learning How To Signal: How To Develop The Skill Of Effective Signaling In A Negotiation In Order To Get The Best Possible Outcome

Miscellaneous

- How To Heal A Broken Leg – Fast!: Understanding how to deal with a broken leg in order to start walking again quickly

- How Software Defined Networking (SDN) Is Going To Change Your World Forever: The Revolution In Network Design And How It Affects

Note: See a complete list of books by Dr. Jim Anderson at the back of this book

Acknowledgements

Any book like this one is the result of years of real-world work experience. In my over 25 years of working for 7 different firms, I have met countless fantastic people and I've been mentored by some truly exceptional ones. Although I've probably forgotten some of the people who made me the person that I am today, here is my attempt to finally give them the recognition that they so truly deserve:

- Thomas P. Anderson
- Art Puett
- Bobbi Marshall
- Bob Boggs

Dr. Jim Anderson

This book is dedicated to my wife Lori. None of this would have been possible without her love and support.

Thanks for the best years of my life (so far)...!

Table Of Contents

MANAGERS WILL ONLY BE AS GOOD AS THEIR TEAM IS 10

ABOUT THE AUTHOR...12

CHAPTER 1: NEW WAYS FOR IT MANAGERS TO KEEP THE STAFF THAT YOU HAVE 17

CHAPTER 2: IT MANAGER SKILLS: THE PROBLEM WITH UNHAPPY IT EMPLOYEES WHO LEAVE 21

CHAPTER 3: WHAT IT MANAGERS NEED TO DO ABOUT BAD APPLES ON THEIR IT TEAM 25

CHAPTER 4: WHY THROWING LEAVING EMPLOYEES UNDER THE BUS IS A BAD IDEA..29

CHAPTER 5: HOW AN IT MANAGER SHOULD PREPARE TO CONDUCT AN INTERVIEW 33

CHAPTER 6: HOW TO USE A DECISION MATRIX AS PART OF THE HIRING PROCESS 37

CHAPTER 7: 10 THINGS IT MANAGERS SHOULD NOT ASK DURING A JOB INTERVIEW 42

CHAPTER 8: 3 HIRING MISTAKES THAT IT MANAGERS MAKE 47

CHAPTER 9: HOW BIG DATA CAN HELP YOU TO BE A BETTER IT MANAGER..51

CHAPTER 10: WHERE DO IT WORKERS COME FROM AND WHAT DO THEY LOOK LIKE?..55

CHAPTER 11: 4 STEPS FOR HIRING THE RIGHT PEOPLE – EVERY TIME 59

CHAPTER 12: 3 WAYS THAT IT MANAGERS CAN DO A BETTER JOB OF HIRING THE RIGHT PERSON 63

Managers Will Only Be As Good As Their Team Is

Any manager is only as good as his or her team. I'm pretty sure that we've all heard this before. However, that leaves us in a bit of a bind – more often than not we are just handed a team and told the make the most of them. However, it turns out that over time we have the ability to reshape and mold our team based on who we choose to add and remove from it. Learning how to do this the right way is what can determine the ultimate success of a manager.

One of the first things that a manager has to realize is that they have got to find ways to keep the team that they have been given. If everyone leaves, you'll not be able to get the work that you are expected to do done. Likewise, if team members become unhappy and then leave that can cause lingering problems for you.

Every team will have their good workers and their bad workers. As a manager you need to be able to spot the bad ones and then you need to come up with a plan for dealing with them. Throwing them under the bus may sound like a good idea, but it turns out that it can have long term consequences.

Hiring new workers is how you will make your team better over time. This means that you need to be able to go into an interview with a plan to determine if this is somebody that you want to add to your team. One way to make sure that you pick the right candidate is to learn how to use a decision matrix.

Managers can make mistakes just like everyone else. However, we need to be careful to not make mistakes when we are hiring someone. Specifically, it turns out that there are things that we must not ask during the hiring process.

New technology is emerging that can help you to be a better manager. The arrival of big data can give you the tools that you need to get more out of your teams. Using this data you may be able to answer the question of where IT workers actually come from. Get good at answering this question and you can start to hire the right people each time.

For more information on what it takes to be a great IT manager, check out my blog, The Accidental IT Leader, at:

www.TheAccidentalITLeader.com

Good luck!

- Dr. Jim Anderson

About The Author

I must confess that I never set out to be a CIO. When I went to school, I studied Computer Science and thought that I'd get a nice job programming and that would be that. Well, at least part of that plan worked out!

My first job was working for Boeing on their F/A-18 fighter jet program. I spent my days programming fighter jet software in assembly language and I loved it. The U.S. government decided to save some money and went looking for other countries to sell this plane to. This put me into an unfamiliar role: I started to meet with foreign military officials and I ended up having to manage groups of engineers who were working on international projects.

Time moved on and so did I. I found myself working for Siemens, the big German telecommunications company. They were making phone switches and selling them to the seven U.S. phone companies. The problem was that the switches were too complicated. Customers couldn't tell the difference between one complicated phone switch from another complicated phone switch. Once again I found myself working with the sales and marketing teams to find ways to make the great technology that the engineers had developed understandable to both internal and external customers.

I've spent over 25 years working as a senior IT professional for both big companies and startups. This has given me an opportunity to learn what it takes to manage and IT department in ways that allow it to maximize its output while becoming a valuable part of the overall company.

I now live in Tampa Florida where I spend my time managing my consulting business, Blue Elephant Consulting, teaching college courses at the University of South Florida, and traveling to work with companies like yours to share the knowledge that I have about how to create and manage successful IT departments.

I'm always available to answer questions and I can be reached at:

Dr. Jim Anderson
Blue Elephant Consulting
Email: jim@BlueElephantConsulting.com
Facebook: http://goo.gl/1TVoK
Web: **www.BlueElephantConsulting.com**

"Unforgettable communication skills that will set your ideas free..."

Create IT Departments That Are Productive And A Valuable Asset To The Rest Of The Company !

Dr. Jim Anderson is available to provide training and coaching on the topics that are the most important to people who have to manage IT departments: how can I build a productive IT department (and keep it together) while at the same time providing the rest of the company with the IT services that they need?

Dr. Anderson believes that in order to both learn and remember what he says, speakers need to laugh. Each one of his speeches is full of fun and humor so that what he says "sticks" with everyone.

Dr. Anderson's CIO Skills Training Includes:

1. How to identify and attract the right type of IT workers to your IT department.
2. How to build relationships with the company's senior management in order to get the support that you need?
3. How to stay on top of changing technology and security issues so that you never get surprised?

Dr. Jim Anderson works with over 100 customers per year. To invite Dr. Anderson to work with you, contact him at:

Phone: 813-418-6970 or
Email: jim@BlueElephantConsulting.com

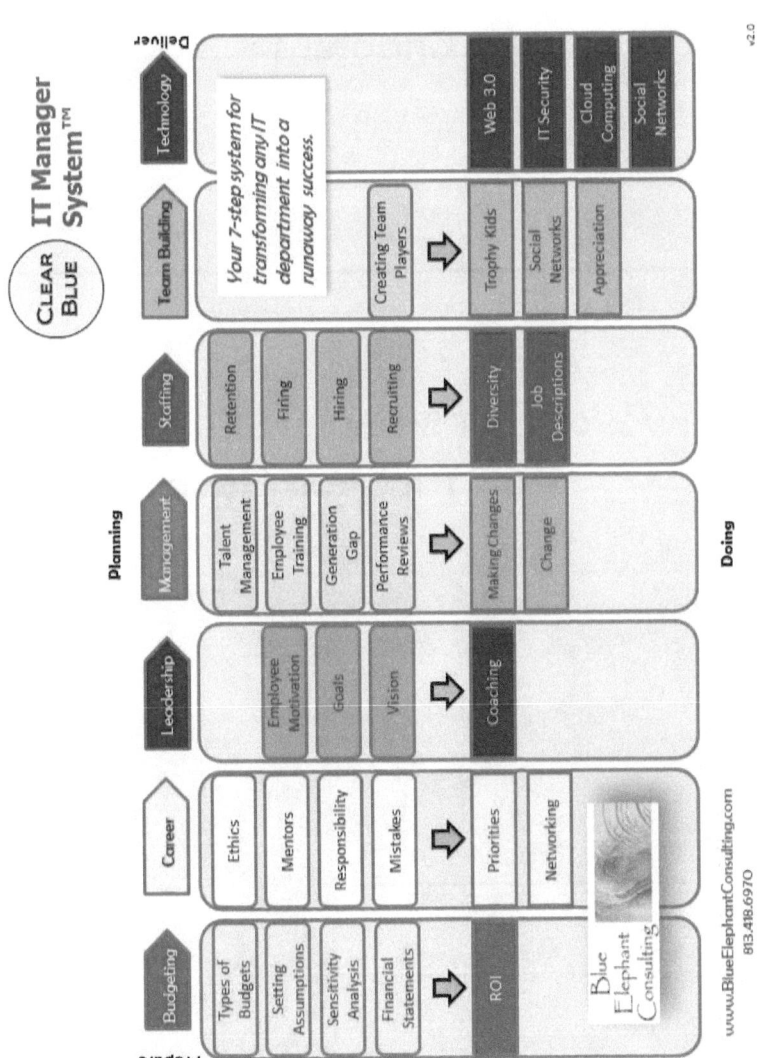

The **Clear Blue IT Manager System™** has been created to provide IT managers with a clear roadmap for how to manage an IT team. This system shows IT Managers what needs to be done and in what order to do it.

Chapter 1

New Ways For Managers To Keep The Staff That You Have

Chapter 1: New Ways For IT Managers To Keep The Staff That You Have

First the bad news: it turns out that 25% of the best workers in the IT department are planning on leaving within the next 12 months. Do I have your attention now? Not to depress you even more, but it turns out that those internal job change programs that are intended to develop the next generation of IT leaders don't work – 40% of the internal rotations that are made by IT "high-pots" (high potential) employees end up in failure. Let's take a look at **what problems you need to solve ...**

Problem: You Aren't Engaging Your Best IT Workers

Jean Martin and Conrad Schmidt are researchers who have been looking into **what makes leadership transitions successful**. What they have discovered is basically bad news for IT managers.

Among the companies that they studied, what they found is that way too many of your IT rising stars are planning on becoming leaders at other firms! Specifically, 25% are currently **planning on leaving your company within one year**, 33% are not fully committed to their job (slackers), 20% have different career goals than they think the company has planned for them, and 40% have little confidence in their coworkers or the company's senior management.

Clearly you have a problem here – **your best & brightest are feeling disengaged**. As an IT manager you need to find ways to get them to reengage with the company and with their careers at your company.

The researchers say that you can get them to both reengage and remain at your company. However, it's going to take **both time and effort on your part**. What you are going to need to do is to provide them with the one thing that they crave above all others – public recognition for the work that they are doing. On top of this, you need to find ways to integrate their actions more closely with the company. This means that the company's goals need to become their goals and you need to find ways to allow them to help tackle the company's biggest challenges.

Problem: High-Pot Doesn't Necessarily Mean Good Leader

Every IT worker wants to be classified as being **a high-potential worker**. What does this really mean? Researchers point out that what a company really wants from its high potential workers are leaders who will be able to grow into larger jobs and then deliver results in those jobs.

Studies have shown that more than 70% of the IT workers who are classified as being "high potential" still **lack critical skills** that will be needed in order be successful in future bigger jobs. What this means for you as an IT manager is that you may be wasting your precious limited talent development budget and resources on the wrong people.

The researchers say that there are three characteristics that an IT manager should be looking for when trying to determine if it would be worthwhile to make further investments in a high-potential team members: **ability, engagement, and aspiration**.

Your best team members need to have both the hard (technical) and soft (management) skills needed **to take on bigger jobs**. Additionally they are going to have be engaged with both the company and its mission – if they don't believe, they won't be willing to help you achieve. Finally, the IT worker's career goals, their aspirations, also need to be in line with what the company is both willing and able to provide them with.

What All Of This Means For You

The job of an IT manager actually has very little to do with technology and everything to do with **developing people**. Not all team members are created the same and IT managers really want to find ways to hold on to their best workers. The problem is that they aren't doing a very good job of this.

In order to keep your best and brightest team members engaged, you are going to have to make a special effort to **recognize them** and work with them to make sure that what they are working on really matters to the company. Likewise, not all high-pots are created equal. Only the ones with ability, true engagement in what the company does, and aspirations that are in line with what the company can offer will be the ones who can grow into true IT leaders.

An IT manager's most important job is to **grow and nurture** the next generation of IT talent that will lead the company's IT teams. In order to do this you are going to have to invest a great deal of your time in ensuring that your best team members don't leave. It is possible to do this, but it needs to become one of your top tasks. If you can do this correctly, then both your career and the company will benefit from it...

Chapter 2

Manager Skills: The Problem With Unhappy Employees Who Leave

Chapter 2: IT Manager Skills: The Problem With Unhappy IT Employees Who Leave

In tough times, every IT manager has seen their share of IT workers **leave the company**. Sometimes they leave because they find a job that they think will be a better fit for them or sometimes the company tells them to leave. No matter what the cause, the one thing that you don't want them to do is leave unhappy. I've got some bad news for you – that's exactly what is happening.

Why You Don't Want Your Employees Leaving Unhappy

A recent survey of workers who had just left their jobs revealed that more than 75% of them **would not recommend the firm** that they had just left to others. This could quickly turn into a big problem for IT managers.

Of course this has always been a problem. However, it has only recently **become a much bigger problem**. Joe Light over at the Wall Street Journal reports that back in 2008, 42% of workers who had just left their job would not recommend the firm that they had just been working for. Clearly this number has grown since then and that's where the problem is coming from.

You might be saying to yourself "So what? They left the company and so of course they are going to have a low opinion of it." No matter what the reason for their leaving was, if they are walking away with bad thoughts about your IT team then it's going to make your IT recruiting efforts **that much harder** to do successfully.

Remember that getting the best and the brightest to come work in your IT team takes two things: you need to have a job opening and **they have to be willing to work for you**. Since IT workers are so well connected, potential new workers often seek out and get advice about accepting a job offer from former employees of a firm. Now do you see the problem?

The reason that former employees are so unhappy is pretty clear. During the most recent economic downturn, most IT workers feel that they got some pretty poor treatment by their IT team. The result of this is that they were left with the feeling that both the company and the IT team **simply didn't care about them**. Therefore, when they leave the company, they have a low opinion about the IT team that they have just separated from.

What You Can Do To Fix This Problem

As an IT manager you need to show some leadership and accept the fact that you are always going to have employees leaving your IT team. No matter if it is because of their decision or because of a downsizing, there will be **a constant outflow** of former employees.

What you can do is to take steps to control how this stream of former IT workers **views the company**. The key is to realize that just because they've left the company doesn't mean that the IT team's relationship with them needs to end.

The most important thing that an IT manager needs to do is to make sure that you **don't lose touch with employees that have left your IT team**. The reason for this is that when it comes time to find new employees, referrals from former employees can be a great way to find the best candidates.

If you are discovering that finding and hiring the right types of IT workers has become difficult, then taking the time to build a network of former IT workers might be well worth the effort.

Hiring candidates that know what they are getting into means that you have a much better chance of them **sticking around** for the long haul.

There is a hidden benefit to taking the time to keep in touch with employees who have left the IT team. It turns out that just because somebody has left doesn't mean that **they won't come back**. Some firms have discovered that between 13-19% of the employees that leave eventually come back. Its numbers like that that can put a smile on a IT manager's face.

What All Of This Means For You

One of the jobs an IT manager does is to attract the best and the brightest IT workers to **come work for your IT dream team** — this is a key management skill. The best way to make this happen is to make sure that the "word on the street" about your company is that it's a great place to work.

If employees are leaving your firm and they are unhappy when they walk out the door, then **you've got a problem**. They'll tell their friends not to go to work for your company. This is going to make recruiting and hiring the best IT workers that much harder to do.

IT managers who realize this can **take action** to ensure that former employees are speaking well of the company by taking the time to stay in touch with high-value employees after they have left the firm. Doing this can often result in them returning or recommending the firm to their friends.

An IT team is only as good as the employees who work in it. It's an IT manager's job to make sure that former employees **talk well of the company** and ensure that recruiting future employees will be that much easier.

Chapter 3

What Managers Need To Do About Bad Apples On Their Team

Chapter 3: What IT Managers Need To Do About Bad Apples On Their IT Team

One of the most important jobs that aN IT manager has to do is to **manage the people that work for him or her**. I'd like to be able to tell you that all of those people are going to be star performers. However, that's not the case. Where an IT manager can run into real problems is when some of the team are bad apples – lazy, angry, or just downright incompetent. What's an IT manager to do?

Why A Bad Apple Is Such A Big Deal

Doesn't every IT team have a few bad apples? Isn't that just something that an IT manager needs to **learn to live with**? Yes, the bad apples exist, but no that's not something that an IT manager needs to live with – it's too expensive.

Robert Sutton has taken a look into **just how expensive bad apples can be**. What he's found is that research has shown that just a single bad apple in a group can bring the group's overall performance down by 30-40%.

It turns out that the behaviors that a bad apple brings to the table, incompetence, anger, and laziness, **are very contagious**. The reason for this is well knows: bad behaviors are stronger than good behaviors. A bad apple causes negative thoughts and feelings to occur in other members of the IT team and these last longer than any positive thoughts or feelings that they may receive from positive coworkers.

What An IT Manager Needs To Do About Bad Apples

The first thing that an IT manager needs to do is to show some leadership and make sure that bad apples don't **find their way into their IT team** in the first place. The concept is simple, it's the execution that can be hard to do.

When you are interviewing someone to come work in your IT team, they may appear to be the perfect candidate. They may have gone to a great school, worked for the best companies, and appear to have just exactly what you are looking for in an IT worker. However, **they may also be a bad apple**.

What you need is some way **to detect that they are a bad apple** before you actually hire them. One way to go about doing this is to invite them to actually come and perform tasks for your company for a day or two.

By having them **perform the work** that you'll be having them do in situations that are realistic, you'll quickly be able to evaluate their personality. You can find out if they are helpful to others and if they know when to ask for help themselves.

If a bad apple does slip by your new employee screening process, then an IT manager needs to **quickly take management action**. There are a number of different options that you have at your disposal. You can try warnings, coaching, and incentives. In the end, you always have the "nuclear option" available to you – physically isolating the bad apple.

Sometimes the bad apple may be one of **your IT stars**. No matter. The damage that a bad apple can do far outshines the value that a star brings to your IT team. Do the right thing and either transform or get rid of your bad apples. Your team will thank you for it.

What All Of This Means For You

Not all IT employees are created equal. Some are stars and **some may be bad apples**. An IT manager needs to take immediate action when a bad apple is detected.

A single bad apple can **hold back an entire team** and reduce their effectiveness. IT managers need to establish screening techniques that will prevent bad apples from being hired in the first place. If a bad apple does somehow get into the IT team, then the IT manager needs to take steps to get them to change – or to leave!

It's always more fun for an IT manager to focus on the star performers in the IT team. However, it turns out that spotting the bad apples and making sure that they **don't get a chance to spoil things** for the rest of the team will go a long way to boosting any IT dream team's productivity!

Chapter 4

Why Throwing Leaving Employees Under The Bus Is A Bad Idea

Chapter 4: Why Throwing Leaving Employees Under The Bus Is A Bad Idea

There you are, an IT manager trying to run an efficient IT team. All of sudden — wham! One of your key team members comes and tells you that **he or she is leaving**. Time to go back the bus up because you've got another soon-to-be-former team member who deserves to be thrown under it. Or maybe not. What's the best way to deal with team members who break up with you?

The Easy Way: A Bad Break-Up

Whenever we feel that a team member has turned against us, our gut reaction is always the same: **I hate you**. They know everything about us and how we run our IT team. We just know that they are going to take all of this secret information and go share it with the competition.

The reality of the modern workplace is that team members who announce that they are leaving **don't leave right off the bat**. Instead they take (or are given) a couple of weeks to wind things down. It's what happens during this time period that can be so damaging to our relationship with them.

The very first thing that happens is that **a distance** immediately starts to grow between us and them. Sure, they're still there, but it's almost as though we are pretending that they aren't. The difficult situation of them getting ready to go on to another job just makes everything worse.

On top of all of this, more often than not, we don't help things out. We go around and **start to bad-mouth the person who is leaving**. We say things like "...we don't really need them..." or "... they didn't really contribute that much..." As with everything that you say, it always finds its way back to the person that you are talking about.

The Right Way: A Good Break-Up

So if our first instinct on how to handle a key team member leaving isn't right, then **what should we really be doing?** This is where you need to show some leadership skills. The first thing that you need to realize is that business is all social. What this means is that our relationships are the most important part about our career.

This means that even if a team member has informed you that they are leaving, it doesn't mean that **your relationship with them is over**. In fact, it's far from it. Your relationship is simply changing – it's going to transform itself into something new and different.

What you want to do at this point in time is to **take charge of the relationship** and make sure that it's going to keep on growing. This starts by sitting down with the leaving team member and coming up with a plan for how they are going to spend their remaining time with the company.

Let them have a lot of say in this plan. You certainly want them to complete as many of the projects that they are working on, but let them tell you what they think that they can accomplish. What's going to be important here is not how much they get done in the time that they have left, but rather **how good they feel about what they've accomplished** when they walk out the door for the last time.

Finally, when it comes time for them to take off, **throw a party**. Use this celebration as a way to congratulate the leaving team member for what they've done and to wish them well as they move on. By doing this you'll have built a relationship that will continue to pay benefits long into the future.

What All Of This Means For You

Managing your staff is one of the key jobs that all IT managers face. Our best laid plans can be thrown into chaos by the announcement of a key IT dream team member's **intended departure**.

How we react to this news is very important. Our initial instinct is going to be to **strike out at that leaving team member**. We tend to isolate them and compound the problem by dismissing their contributions when we talk with others.

What we need to be doing is realizing that **relationships are more important than anything else that we do as IT manager**. That means that even when a team member announces that they are leaving, it doesn't mean that our relationship with them is ending. Rather it's preparing to transform. We need to show good management skills and take steps to make sure that this is a positive transformation.

IT managers who are able to do the right thing will be able to **build a strong network of social relationships**. The ability to build this network using both current and former team members is what sets the great IT managers apart from everyone else!

Chapter 5

How A Manager Should Prepare To Conduct An Interview

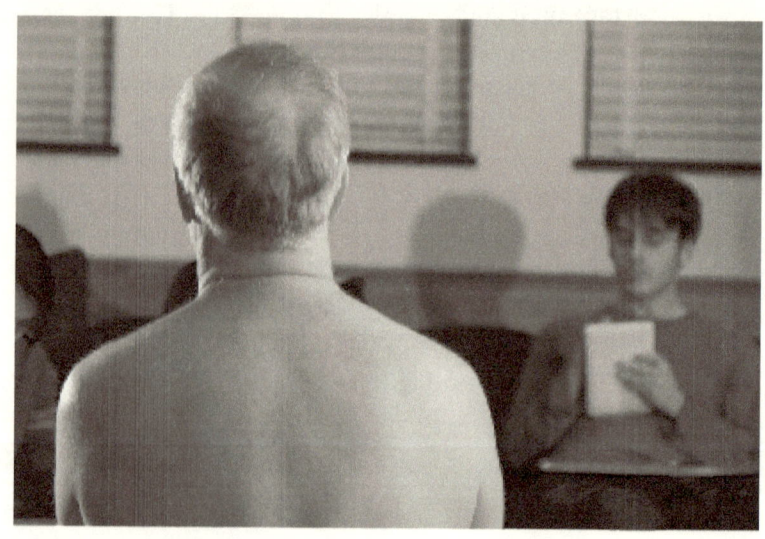

Chapter 5: How An IT Manager Should Prepare To Conduct An Interview

Those pesky job interviews – management always seems to put them on your to-do list just when you have a million other things to do. Yes, they are important, I mean after all who you hire will shape your IT team for years to come. However, when you are pressed for time, **what's the best way for an IT manager to go about preparing for one of these things?**

What's The Job All About?

If you think about it, you really can't hope to conduct a successful job interview if you don't have **a good understanding of just exactly what tasks the company is looking to have performed**. That means that you've got some homework to do.

The first thing that you're going to want to do is to **review the job profile**. The result of your doing this should be that you are able to create a list of the key responsibilities and tasks that the person who is filling the role will have to perform.

As we all know, being a member of an IT dream team **requires a number of different skill sets**. This means that you need to come up with a list of any training that would be required in order to perform this job. Additionally you are going to want to understand if there are any experiences or personal attributes that would allow the person who is applying for the job be more successful.

How To Explore What The Candidate Has To Offer

Every interview consists of you asking the candidate a series of questions. It's going to be **how they answer these questions** and what they say that will lead you to making a decision about your willingness to allow them to join your IT team. This means that you're going to need to come up with a way to record not only the questions that you've asked them, but also their answers.

The first step is for you to take the time before the interview and **identify each of the areas that you are going to want to explore with them**. These areas should be related to what the candidate will be expected to do for the company.

You are going to want to **create several questions** that you'll ask the candidate about each of these areas. Make sure that you take the time during the interview to record their response to each question. You'd be amazed at how little you'll be able to remember once the interview is done.

Finally, once the interview is over and the candidate has left, **you need to rank them**. It's best to do this as close to the actual interview time as possible so that your memory is freshest. Rank each candidate according to how they did in each of key areas. You'll use these rankings to compare candidates when all of the interviews have been concluded.

What All Of This Means For You

As the global economy starts to improve, companies are once again **starting to interview candidates to join their IT teams**. You'll probably be called on to conduct some of these interviews and that means that you are going to have to show some leadership and prepare to do it.

When you are preparing to conduct the interview, you're going to have to make sure that you have a **full understanding** of just what the job requires. Once you know this, you'll need to create specific questions in order to explore what the candidate has to offer.

Selecting the right candidate to join your IT team is perhaps the most important part of being an IT manager. The person that you select may be a part of your team **for many years**. Take the time to do it correctly, and you'll have an IT team that you can be proud of.

Chapter 6

How To Use A Decision Matrix As Part Of The Hiring Process

Chapter 6: How To Use A Decision Matrix As Part Of The Hiring Process

This **hiring of new members for your IT team** can be very difficult to do at times even though it is one of the critical IT manager skills. The problem comes up when you've interviewed a group of qualified candidates. Now comes the hard part: how do you choose the right one for your team?

What Goes Into A Hiring Decision Matrix

When you are faced with a collection of very talented candidates who are all vying for the same spot on your team, you've got a problem on your hands that there is no IT manager training for. What you need to do is to **use a hiring decision matrix** in order to sort through each of the candidates and determine which one is going to be the right one to add to your team.

A hiring decision matrix consists of both rows and columns. You'll create a row for each one of the candidates that you are going to be interviewing for the position. You'll ultimate goal here is going to be to build a matrix that will permit you to **compare each candidate to each other** in order to determine who is the best suited to be added to your team.

Next comes the columns. Each of the columns that you create in your matrix will relate to the characteristics that you believe are needed **in order to successful in this job**. Ultimately you are going to have to be the one who determines what the correct columns to use are; however, I can provide you with some helpful suggestions here.

One very good way to compare candidates is to include a column that identified their **education level**. You may also want to include notes on what school(s) they attended just in case everyone has the same level of education.

Two more columns that are helpful are **previous experiences and job accomplishments**. It's not just the jobs that each candidate has worked at that are important, but also what they feel as though they were able to accomplish while they were spending their time there.

Next come the **skills & knowledge** and the personal attributes columns. Skills & knowledge are critical in determining how quickly each candidate will be able to start to be a productive member of your team. The personal attributes column may be more subjective, but it should provide you with a feel for how well this candidate will get along with the rest of your current team.

The final column is the **previous appraisal or rating** column. You'll never be able to be aware of everything that has happened in each candidate's past work experiences. That's why asking them questions about how their past job performance was rated is a great way to try to capture some of the knowledge that their previous boss had.

How To Use A Hiring Decision Matrix

Just building a hiring decision matrix isn't good enough: now you are going to have to **use it to make a hiring decision**. One important point to be aware of here is that this tool is not a magic tool – it's not necessarily going to clearly show you which candidate you should pick. Instead, view it as allowing you to discard all but two of your candidates.

For each one of the columns that you've created, you are going to want to **rank each of your interview candidates**. I would suggest using a scale that runs from 1 (poor) to 10 (excellent).

Once you've ranked each candidate, you can then add up their individual scores and create a single score for each person.

Generally what you are going to find is **clusters**. You'll have a couple of candidate at the top end of your scale, a few in the middle, and one or two at the bottom. You can now discard the middle and the bottom and just focus on the top end candidates.

You are now done using the hiring decision matrix – it's accomplished what it was designed for. Now you need to **use your IT manager skills** and make a tough decision. What you are going to want to do is to reflect on how the interviews went and make a decision on exactly which candidate you felt was the best match for joining your team.

What All Of This Means For You

Under the best of circumstances, hiring someone to join your IT team can be **a challenging task** and should be considered to be yet another part of the critical task of IT team building. When you are faced with a number of candidates that are all very well qualified, it becomes even more difficult.

In order to make the process of making the right selection easier, IT managers can **create and use a hiring decision matrix**. This matrix consists of an individual row for each candidate. Individual columns are then created based on the characteristics that you have identified as being required in order to perform the job. Ultimately the decision matrix will provide you with guidance that will help finding the answer to the question of who to hire; however, you will still need to use your own best judgment.

The makeup of your IT team is a critical factor in determining the team's chances of being successful. As an IT manager, you need to transform what is all too often **a gut decision** into a process that will make sure that you make the right decision. Using a hiring decision matrix will eliminate some of the chance in this process and will help you to make the right hiring decisions.

Chapter 7

10 Things Managers Should NOT Ask During A Job Interview

Chapter 7: 10 Things IT Managers Should NOT Ask During A Job Interview

As IT managers sometimes we tend to think that we know it all – that we have all of the IT manager skills that we need. This can be dangerous, especially when it comes to conducting job interviews. If you don't have the right IT manager training then what goes on during a job interview **just might land both you and your company in court** and that's something that nobody wants. Let's take a look at what you must never say during a job interview.

10 Things To Never Ask During A Job Interview

As IT managers we are **naturally curious** about anyone who has applied to join our team. Why do they want to join? What have they done in the past? Who are they? These are all natural questions; however, rules and regulations have been established to limit the types of questions that we can ask when interviewing a candidate for a job.

Although none of us likes to feel as though a conversation that we are going to be having **is restricted in any way**, it turns out that the rules surrounding job interviews are actually a good thing. What everyone is trying to avoid is having a job candidate be rejected for the wrong reasons – things have nothing to do with their ability to perform the job.

So **what can't you talk about** during a job interview? It turns out that anything having to do with a person's physical nature, their religious or political beliefs, or where they came from are all off limits. Just to get a bit more granular, here are 10 topics that you need to steer clear of during your next job interview:

Age: This is a big red flag – many companies have been sued because a job applicant believed that they were turned down because they were too old. Don't try to get clever and ask questions about what year they were born in, that's the same thing as asking how old they are.

Religion: This is a bit tricky. You cannot ask about someone's religion and you can't ask them if they are going to take time off for their religious holidays. However, you can say that " ...this job requires you to work over the weekend sometimes, do you have any responsibilities that would conflict with this requirement?" Note that this question has nothing to do with religion.

Marital Status: If someone is married, divorced, or not married that should have nothing to do with their ability to perform the job that they are interviewing for. This means you need to stay away from these questions and not ask roundabout questions like "what does your husband / wife do for a living?"

Children: Asking about children is a natural part of any conversation that we often have with someone when we are meeting them for the first time. However, you need to stay away from this one during a job interview. Don't even ask questions about any child care arrangements that they might have to make if they got the job – that's the same as if you asked if they had children.

Race: Hopefully I don't have to tell you that asking any questions about race is off limits. This can sometimes slip into a conversation if an applicant is of a mixed race – their background can be a normal conversation topic. Make sure that you don't go there. Additionally, in this era of digital images, make sure that submitting a photo is not a part of any job interview. It would be too easy to say that you had discriminated against a job candidate based on what you saw in their photo.

Gender / Sexual Orientation: Clearly off limits. In this day and age, the number of possible sexual orientations that a job candidate might have has become a very long list. This has nothing to do with how well they could perform the job that you are interviewing them for and so don't ask about it.

National Origin: What country a candidate was born in or where they are from is not something that you should discuss during a job interview. This can be a tricky one to avoid. Don't ask about where a last name came from or where their parents grew up.

Citizenship: Unless the job that the candidate is interviewing for requires specific citizenship, stay away from this one. The good news here is that you can ask the question "If hired, are you legally authorized to work in this country?"

Handicap: Careful here. Even if the candidate's handicap is very obvious, you can't ask any questions about it. Keep in mind that a handicap may not be obvious. It could be physical, mental, or it could be related to alcoholism, drug addiction, or even AIDS. A valid question to ask would go like this "Would you be able to perform the essential functions of this job with or without reasonable accommodations?"

Arrests: You might find this one just a bit strange, but unless the candidate is applying for a security related job, you are not permitted to ask them any questions about prior arrests or convictions.

What All Of This Means For You

Finding the right person to join your team, just like doing IT team building, is a tough job. The job interview is your one chance to really probe and discover if they have what it is going to take in order to be a successful member of your team. However, **danger lurks during any job interview**.

During a job interview with a prospective candidate, an IT manager needs to be very careful to **stay away from** any questions that have to do with the candidate's personal life. Instead, all of your questions need to have a laser like focus on the duties associated with the position that you are trying to fill and the professional skills that this candidate will be able to apply to the job.

All of the rules and laws that surround the job interview process may seem like a burden some of the time. However, it turns out that these rules are in place to help you out as much as they are there to help the candidate out. By keeping your questions focused on what really matters, **how the candidate would do the job**, you'll become a better interviewer and you'll end up hiring better team members.

Chapter 8

3 Hiring Mistakes That Managers Make

Chapter 8: 3 Hiring Mistakes That IT Managers Make

When a IT Manager makes a hiring decision, **it can have a long lasting impact on the team**. This means that the IT Manager wants use their IT manager skills and take his or her time when considering candidates and not make a foolish blunder. However, all too often we select the wrong person for the wrong job. Looking back at our hiring mistakes, more often than not it turns out that we made one of the three most common mistakes that IT Managers make when hiring someone.

Not Preparing For The Interview

Let's face it – IT Managers never have enough time. However, when it comes to evaluating people that we're thinking about hiring, **we need to find the time to do the job properly**. This should really be a part of our basic IT manager training. All too often, we'll bring a candidate's resume along with us to the interview and read it for the first time while we're sitting with them. This is no way to conduct an interview. As the IT Manager, you need to do your homework. Read the resume before the interview, follow up with any references and create a list of questions that you're going to want to get answers to.

Not Getting Referrals

Unless you have the ability to see into the future, you're not going to be able to determine how well a candidate is going to work out in your IT team if you choose to hire them. It always comes down to making an educated guess. However, you can improve your odds of guessing correctly if you allow your good employees to make recommendations about who you should be interviewing for an open position. Every study that has been done has confirmed that **good employees make good recommendations**.

Setting Too High Of A Bar

New home buyers always make the same mistake: they create a list of everything that they want in a house and then they go looking for that "perfect house" that has everything on their wish list. IT Managers can act the same way when they are trying to fill a position on their team. If they have a list of 10 skills or experiences that they want the candidate to have, then they're not willing to hire the person who has 8 of them and good social skills. Understand that **you'll never get everything that you want** and pick the next closest candidate.

What All Of This Means For You

The real value of any IT team comes not from any IT team building that you have your team do, but rather from the people who work on it. Every hire that a IT Manager makes is going to have **a long lasting impact on the team** and so we want to take our time and make the right decision. However, it can be all too easy to make one of three different common hiring mistakes when it's time to make this important decision.

Considering how important each hire that the person in the IT Manager position makes, you would think that they would **do their homework** on each candidate. However, all too often we don't take the time to prepare for the interview. Since we have limited time to talk with any candidate, having our existing good employees make recommendations would make our hiring job a lot easier. Finally, you'll never get everything that you want in a single candidate so IT Managers have to prioritize what they are looking for.

The value of making the right hiring decision is that with a little luck **you won't have to revisit making the same decision for quite some time**. If you make the wrong decision because you made one of these three mistakes then you'll be repeating the hiring process far too soon. Take the time to make sure that these are mistakes that you don't make the next time that you hire for your IT team!

Chapter 9

How Big Data Can Help You To Be A Better Manager

Chapter 9: How Big Data Can Help You To Be A Better IT Manager

As IT managers, our IT manager skills include the hiring, promotion, and career planning of the members of our team. All too often, we end up making decisions in this area based on what little IT manager training we've had and **our "gut feel"** about what is right for our team. In the field of human resource management, the power of big data processing is starting to be applied to all of that employee data that we've been collecting for so long. What's being discovered just might change how you manage your team...

What You Know Is Wrong

A lot of the things that your gut might be telling you about how to be a better IT manager might just **turn out to be flat out wrong**. Specifically, a lot of the time we IT managers wonder if we really matter? Do our team members only hang around if they have challenging work, if they are paid more than at other firms, or if the company offers them the occasional free lunch? The answer is no. Recent studies have shown that how a worker interacts with their manager makes a huge difference on their decision to stay in a job or move on.

Likewise, does it really matter if a job candidate that you are interviewing has had 5 jobs in the last 2 years? Or does it matter if they've been out of a job for the past 18 months? Crunching the numbers using big data analytics processing has revealed that a person's previous employment history really has **nothing to do with how long they are going to remain at your company**. A job candidate's previous work history turns to not be a good predictor of the results that you'll have with them.

Finally, when it comes to IT team members that you need to go out and sell the services that your team has to offer to other departments, you would think that you'd want to pick the ones who have **the most outgoing personalities** – the ones who look the most like a traditional sales person, right? It turns out that this is not the case. What you really should be looking for is the member of your team who has what is called "emotional courage". This person is going to be able to keep persisting even after they've been initially told "no" by another department.

Lessons From Google

If there is any company out there in the world of IT that we would expect to be **using big data** to improve how they deal with their IT teams, it would be Google. It turns out that they have not let us down.

When Google initially started out, they knew that they wanted to hire only the best and the brightest candidates. They did exactly what the rest of us IT managers do: they decided to make their hiring decisions based on a candidate's SAT scores and college grade-point average. Google has collected a great deal of data on its employees and they've found that this method **has not been a good predictor** of who will turn into a good Google employee.

Based on the employee surveys that Google has been doing since 2007 Google has discovered what type of IT worker seems to be the happiest working there. The characteristic that determines employee happiness at Google is **how innovative they are**. Those workers who have a strong sense of mission about the work that they are doing and feel that they have a great deal of personal autonomy about how they do this work are the ones who stay the longest, participate in IT team building, and who are the most productive.

What All Of This Means For You

IT managers who want to both build and maintain the best IT team possible are going to have to learn to overcome some of the **gut-based decisions** that they've been relying on in the past. A better solution is needed.

The arrival of big data and its associated analytical functions is for the first time allowing the field of human resource management to have **a rigorous scientific method** applied to it. A lot of the things that we IT managers have always assumed to be true are now turning out to be incorrect.

Over at Google they used to try to hire the best and the brightest college graduates based on their SAT and grade point average scores. Having conducted numerous surveys of their employees, what they've discovered is that having a sense of innovation is much more important to a Google employee's **long term success**.

As IT managers we need to take the time to collect all of the data that we can on our IT team members. Hidden within this data are **the answers to the questions that we should be asking** about who we should hire and how we can keep our best workers. Take the time to collect the big data, and you just might be surprised what you discover!

Chapter 10

Where Do Workers Come From And What Do They Look Like?

Chapter 10: Where Do IT Workers Come From And What Do They Look Like?

As an IT manager, you are responsible for having the IT manager skills needed to build the IT teams that will be able to solve your company's toughest problems. However, do you know where to look for the people that you'll want to add to your team? None of us have ever had any IT manager training in how to do this. For that matter, **do you even know what you are looking for?** Here's a hint: they are not going to look like you! Let's have a chat about where today's IT workers are coming from and what they look like…

What Do Today's IT Workers Look Like?

The first question that IT managers need to answer is **just exactly what do today's IT workers look like?** I'm going to focus on system administrators because they are harder to find. This question has three different components to it: gender, race, and age.

The first question, gender, is probably one that we all know how to answer very well. The majority of IT workers, system administrators specifically, **are male**. In fact, a whopping 75% the IT staff that you probably have are male. However, the 25% that are women is growing and so you need to keep your eyes open for opportunities to add more women to your team.

When it comes to race, I was quite surprised to discover that **68% of IT workers are white**. After that, the next largest segment is the Asian segment at 11%. This is followed closely by the Hispanic segment at 10.7% and the black segment at 10%.

Finally, when it comes to age of system administrators, I was once again surprised to discover how old the IT industry is. The **largest segment of IT workers** are 35-44 years old and this makes up 36% of the industry. The next largest segment is the 25-34 segment which contains 31%. The final segment of any significant size consists of workers who are 45-54 years old and this makes up 17% of the market.

Where Do They Come From?

Now that we know what a typical IT worker looks like, the next big question is **where do they come from?** One of the biggest questions is do these workers have university degrees. When you take a look at how much effort most companies put into recruiting on college campuses, you would assume that they all do.

However, that assumption would be wrong. In a recent survey done by the Wall Street Journal, it turns out that **only 40% of IT workers have a bachelor's university degree**. The next largest segment is those workers who have some university education, but who never got a bachelor's degree. This group consists of 25% of IT workers.

There are, of course, other levels of education represented in IT. **16% of IT workers have received an associate's degree**. This is followed by 10% who have gone on to get a master's degree. Clearly the level of education that you'll find when you are looking to add to your IT team will be all over the map.

What Does This Mean For You?

One of the biggest mistakes that an IT manager can make is to **assume that he or she knows what IT workers look like**. We've all formed our own opinions based on who we attended university with and who we've worked with during our career. However, that may not accurately reflect who we should be looking at to add to our IT teams today. Remember: you can't do any IT team building until you have built your team!

Today's IT workers are primarily white males. However, there is **a growing representation** from both women and minorities. The majority of IT workers are over 35 years old. However, that may change as the baby boomers start to retire. Somewhere between 33-40% of IT workers will have a university degree.

It is critical that IT managers understand what they are looking for when they go to staff their team. The IT workers of yesterday **don't look anything like the IT workers of today**. Make sure that you stay on top of what IT workers both look like and where they come from. This is the only way that you'll be able to build IT teams that will be successful!

Chapter 11

4 Steps For Hiring The Right People – Every Time

NOW HIRING

Chapter 11: 4 Steps For Hiring The Right People – Every Time

As an IT manager, one of your most important jobs is to hire the right people to join your IT team. The ability to do this correctly is one of our critical IT manager skills, but too few of us have ever received any IT manager training on how to do it correctly. IT managers will often try to perform this job **based on their "gut feel"**. What we all need to understand is that hiring the right people is a process. If we follow the right process, then we'll get the right people – every time.

The Hiring Process

All too often **we fail to create any sort of process** for getting to know the person that we are considering inviting to join our team. Instead, we grab a copy of their resume just before the interview happens and head off to use what we think has worked for us in the past. Bad idea.

Instead, **what we need is a process**. The goal of this process has to be to uncover if the person that we are talking with would be a good fit for the company, the job, and your team. One way to create process that works would be to use the following four steps:

Ditch The "Silver Bullets": There is no such thing as a magical interview question. We have all heard about places like Google and Microsoft in which the interview process contains so-called curveball questions like "how many golf balls could you fit on a school bus". These questions really don't serve any purpose and the candidate knows all about them so you are not going to be getting any useful information from them when you use this type of question.

Know What You Want: All too often we enter into the hiring process with a vague or ill-formed understanding of just exactly what type of person and skill set we are looking for. You can't do this. Instead, you need to make sure that you have a crystal clear understanding of exactly what you are looking for in terms of skills, attitudes, and behaviors in the perfect candidate. Take the time to talk to people who've had the job before and find out what it's going to take for the next person to be successful.

Prove It: Some candidates can talk a good line. By listening to them you'll come away with the impression that they've "been there, done that". Don't believe what you are hearing. Instead, always ask for proof. For hard skills, have them do whatever they say that they can do. For soft skills, put them in a situation where they can show you how good their soft skills are. Make sure that you are buying what you really think that you are buying.

Don't Do It Alone: Hiring is a difficult process. Don't try to pull this off all by yourself. Instead, involve other people. In order to hire the right person, it takes perspective. Always try to involve at least two people in the interviewing process and try to expose the candidate to the people that they would be working with in order to get their feedback. The more inputs that you are able to collect, the better the chances that you'll make the right hiring decision are.

What All Of This Means For You

An IT manager has the responsibility to **correctly staff their IT team**. This is about more than just doing some IT team building, it all starts with you needing to know how to go about hiring the right people. Forget about going with your "gut feel" and instead implement a process that will deliver to you the right person for the job each and every time.

This process has to be based on fact. Ditch the clever silver bullet questions – they never work. Make sure that you know what you are looking for – you'll never find it if you don't. However, never take the candidate's word for it, instead verify that they have what it takes to do the job. You can only do so much, **make sure that you've got back up on this task** and get their input as the process moves forward.

The good news is that you can avoid hiring the wrong candidates and you can hire the right ones. The bad news is that this is never easy to do. Take the time to **implement a hiring process that works** and you'll find that your IT team has been staffed with all the right people.

Chapter 12

3 Ways That Managers Can Do A Better Job Of Hiring The Right Person

NOW HIRING

Chapter 12: 3 Ways That IT Managers Can Do A Better Job Of Hiring The Right Person

IT Managers realize that **your success rests firmly on the shoulders of those people who are on your team.** What this means is that the process of hiring someone is one of your a critical IT manager skills. Hire the right person and you'll move forward, hire the wrong person and you may stumble or even be asked to leave the firm. How can you go about doing this correctly?

Interview People, Of Course

In all honesty, the interview is the least effective way of finding out if a candidate is the right person for a job. The reason for this is that, of course, **they are on their best behavior during the interview.** If they are good at hiding their flaws then you'll never be able to detect it during the short time that you sit and talk with them. There is nothing in our IT manager training that will allow us to get more out of an interview.

All too often we end up making our hiring decisions based on our human judgment. The problem with this is that **all too often, we're wrong.** There can be a number of different reasons for this, but the biggest one that I've found is that when I meet someone new I end up mapping them to someone that I already know. This can end up hiding a lot of the new person's faults.

Considering how important this new person is going to be to your career, **you'd really like to have a chance to get inside of their head.** However, during an interview all you have to go on is what they chose to put on their resume. In the end, you just can't find out what you need to know about the person during an interview.

Simulate The Job

A much better way to determine if someone is the right person for the job is to **have them actually do the job**. There is no other way that a faker will be exposed than to ask them to actually perform the work that you are thinking about hiring them to do.

Let the candidate know **what issues your IT team is currently facing** and then let them simulate performing the job that you are hiring for. We are not talking about something that can be accomplished in 30 minutes. Rather we are talking about something that is going to take from 8-40 hours to complete. Yes, that's an investment, but considering how important finding the right person is I think that it's worth it.

Ultimately, you're going to walk away from this exercise **with a better feel for if this person is the right person for the job**. The flip side is that they will also have a much better understanding of what the job is going to entail. If it turns out that they no longer want the job, then they will have saved both of you a lot of pain and suffering by walking away.

Check Out Off-List References

References are something that I believe are a very important part of the hiring process. However, in this day and age **I don't think that we spend enough time checking them out**. Most resumes have between one and three references listed on them; however, these are generally useless.

The reason that they are useless is because the candidate has already talked with these people and gotten them to **agree to say only nice things about him or her**. In order to determine what type of person your candidate really is, you are going to have to dig deeper.

This means that you are going to have to find and talk with **off-list references**. This means that you are going to want to find other people who have worked with this person and get their real impressions of them. Use your network of friends and associates to find these people. This way when you find them, they'll feel obligated to provide you with an honest assessment of your candidate.

What Does All Of This Mean For You?

No matter how well you understand IT team building, that's not what is going to make you a successful IT Manager. Instead, **it's the quality of the team that you are able to build** that is going to determine your eventual success as an IT manager. This means that you need to learn how to pick the right people.

In order to fully evaluate the candidate for a job, you will, of course, need to start out by conducting a traditional interview. Next you'll want to provide the candidate with an opportunity to **actually perform the job**. Finally, take the time to check out references that they didn't provide you with.

There's no doubt that you can be successful as an IT manager. However, you're going to have to **master the art of hiring the right people**. In order to do this you'll need to learn how to use these three tips to make sure that you invite the right people to join your team.

It's from the forge of failure that the steel of success is formed.

Hard Work Does Not Guarantee Success, But Success Does Not Happen Without Hard Work.

— Dr. Jim Anderson

Create IT Departments That Are Productive And A Valuable Asset To The Rest Of The Company!

Dr. Jim Anderson is available to provide training and coaching on the topics that are the most important to people who have to manage IT departments: how can I build a productive IT department (and keep it together) while at the same time providing the rest of the company with the IT services that they need?

Dr. Anderson believes that in order to both learn and remember what he says, speakers need to laugh. Each one of his speeches is full of fun and humor so that what he says "sticks" with everyone.

Dr. Anderson's CIO Skills Training Includes:

1. How to identify and attract the right type of IT workers to your IT department.
2. How to build relationships with the company's senior management in order to get the support that you need?
3. How to stay on top of changing technology and security issues so that you never get surprised?

Dr. Jim Anderson works with over 100 customers per year. To invite Dr. Anderson to work with you, contact him at:

Phone: 813-418-6970 or
Email: jim@BlueElephantConsulting.com

Blue Elephant Consulting
Speaking. Negotiating. Managing. Marketing.

Photo Credits:

Cover - Photo by rawpixel on Unsplash

https://unsplash.com/photos/kyRiEW0S7FY?utm_source=unsplash&utm_medium=referral&utm_content=creditCopyText

Chapter 1 – xpistwv

https://morguefile.com/p/156790

Chapter 2 - Nicki Dugan Pogue

https://www.flickr.com/photos/thenickster/

Chapter 3 – Dreamstime

https://www.dreamstime.com/royalty-free-stock-photography-bad-teeth-image2011957

Chapter 4 – dantada

https://morguefile.com/p/66661

Chapter 5 - Quinn Dombrowski

https://www.flickr.com/photos/quinnanya/4272985057/

Chapter 6 – Visionello

https://www.flickr.com/photos/visionello/4458183538/

Chapter 7 - Ted Murphy

https://www.flickr.com/photos/tedmurphy/5125677289/

Chapter 8 - Terrance Heath

https://www.flickr.com/photos/terrancedc/

Chapter 9 - Pamlau

https://www.flickr.com/photos/pamlau/5723491286/

Chaptewr 10 - David Nichols

https://www.flickr.com/photos/mybluevan/

Chapter 11 - Nathan Stephens

https://www.flickr.com/photos/groundswellzoo/with/8272206292/

Chapter 12 - Nathan Stephens

https://www.flickr.com/photos/groundswellzoo/with/8272206292/

Other Books By The Author

Product Management

- Developing World Class Products: Techniques For Product Managers To Better Understand What Their Customers Really Want

- How Product Managers Can Sell More Of Their Product: Tips & Techniques For Product Managers To Better Understand How To Sell Their Product

- How Product Managers Can Sell More Of Their Product: Tips & Techniques For Product Managers To Better Understand How To Sell Their Product

- How To Create A Successful Product That Customers Will Want: Techniques For Product Managers To Boost Product Sales And Increase Customer Satisfaction

- What Product Managers Need To Know About World-Class Product Development: How Product Managers Can Create Successful Products

- How Product Managers Can Learn To Understand Their Customers: Techniques For Product

Managers To Better Understand What Their Customers Really Want

- Product Management Secrets: Techniques For Product Managers To Boost Product Sales And Increase Customer Satisfaction

- Product Development Lessons For Product Managers: How Product Managers Can Create Successful Products

- Customer Lessons For Product Managers: Techniques For Product Managers To Better Understand What Their Customers Really Want

- Product Failure Lessons For Product Managers: Examples Of Products That Have Failed For Product Managers To Learn From

- Communication Skills For Product Managers: The Communication Skills That Product Managers Need To Know How To Use In Order To Have A Successful Product

- How To Have A Successful Product Manager Career: The Things That You Need To Be Doing TODAY In Order To Have A Successful Product Manager Career

- Product Manager Product Success: How to keep your product on track and make it become a success

Public Speaking

- Unforgettable Presentations That Can Change The World: Presentation techniques that will transform a speech into a memorable event

- Creating Speeches That Work: How To Create A Speech That Will Make Your Message Be Remembered Forever!

- How To Organize A Speech In Order To Make Your Point: How to put together a speech that will capture and hold your audience's attention

- Changing How You Speak To Overcome Your Fear Of Speaking: Change techniques that will transform a speech into a memorable event

- Delivering Excellence: How To Give Presentations That Make A Difference: Presentation techniques that will transform a speech into a memorable event

- Tools Speakers Need In Order To Give The Perfect Speech: What tools to use to create your next speech so that your message will be remembered forever!

- How To Create A Speech That Will Be Remembered

- Secrets To Organizing A Speech For Maximum Impact: How to put together a speech that will capture and hold your audience's attention

- How To Become A Better Speaker By Changing How You Speak: Change techniques that will transform a speech into a memorable event

- How To Give A Great Presentation: Presentation techniques that will transform a speech into a memorable event

- How To Rehearse In Order To Give The Perfect Speech: How to effectively rehearse your next speech to that your message be remembered forever!

- Secrets To Creating The Perfect Speech: How to create a speech that will make your message be remembered forever!

- Secrets To Organizing The Perfect Speech: How to organize the best speech of your life!

- Secrets To Planning The Perfect Speech: How to plan to give the best speech of your life

- How To Show What You Mean During A Presentation: How to use visual techniques to transform a speech into a memorable event

CIO Skills

- Communication Skills That Every CIO Must Have: Tips And Techniques For CIOs To Use In Order To Become Better Communicators

- How CIOs Can Bring Business And IT Together: How CIOs Can Use Their Technical Skills To Help Their Company Solve Real-World Business Problems

- New IT Technology Issues Facing CIOs: How CIOs Can Stay On Top Of The Changes In The Technology That Powers The Company

- Keeping The Barbarians Out: How CIOs Can Secure Their Department and Company: Tips And Techniques For CIOs To Use In Order To Secure Both Their IT Department And Their Company

- What CIOs Need To Know In Order To Successfully Manage An IT Department: Decision Making Skills That Every CIO Needs To Have In Order To Be Able To Make The Right Choices

- Becoming A Powerful And Effective Leader: Tips And Techniques That IT Managers Can Use In Order To Develop Leadership Skills

- CIO Secrets For Growing Innovation: Tips And Techniques For CIOs To Use In Order To Make Innovation Happen In Their IT Department

- Your Success As A CIO Depends On How Well You Communicate: Tips And Techniques For CIOs To Use In Order To Become Better Communicators

- What CIOs Need To Know About Working With Partners: Techniques For CIOs To Use In Order To Be Able To Successfully Work With Partners

- Critical CIO Management Skills: Decision Making Skills That Every CIO Needs To Have In Order To Be Able To Make The Right Choices

- How CIOs Can Make Innovation Happen: Tips And Techniques For CIOs To Use In Order To Make Innovation Happen In Their IT Department

- CIO Communication Skills Secrets: Tips And Techniques For CIOs To Use In Order To Become Better Communicators

- Managing Your CIO Career: Steps That CIOs Have To Take In Order To Have A Long And Successful

Career

- CIO Business Skills: How CIOs can work effectively with the rest of the company!

IT Manager Skills

- How IT Managers Can Use New Technology To Meet Today's IT Challenges: Technologies That IT Managers Can Use In Order to Make Their Teams More Productive

- How To Build High Performance IT Teams: Tips And Techniques That IT Managers Can Use In Order To Develop Productive Teams

- Save Yourself, Save Your Job – How To Manage Your IT Career: Secrets That IT Managers Can Use In Order To Have A Successful Career

- Growing Your CIO Career: How CIOs Can Work With The Entire Company In Order To Be Successful

- How IT Managers Can Make Innovation Happen: Tips And Techniques For IT Managers To Use In Order To Make Innovation Happen In Their Teams

- Staffing Skills IT Managers Must Have: Tips And Techniques That IT Managers Can Use In Order To

Correctly Staff Their Teams

- Secrets Of Effective Leadership For IT Managers: Tips And Techniques That IT Managers Can Use In Order To Develop Leadership Skills

- IT Manager Career Secrets: Tips And Techniques That IT Managers Can Use In Order To Have A Successful Career

- IT Manager Budgeting Skills: How IT Managers Can Request, Manage, Use, And Track Their Funding

- Secrets Of Managing Budgets: What IT Managers Need To Know In Order To Understand How Their Company Uses Money

Negotiating

- The Art Of Packaging A Negotiation: How To Develop The Skill Of Assembling Potential Trades In Order To Get The Best Possible Outcome

- Getting What You Want In A Negotiation By Learning How To Signal: How To Develop The Skill Of Effective Signaling In A Negotiation In Order To Get The Best Possible Outcome

- Exploring How To Get The Deal That You Want In A Negotiation: How To Develop The Skill Of Exploring

What Is Possible In A Negotiation In Order To Reach The Best Possible Deal

- Use The Power Of Arguing To Win Your Next Negotiation: How To Develop The Skill Of Effective Arguing In A Negotiation In Order To Get The Best Possible Outcome

- Learn How To Signal In Your Next Negotiation: How To Develop The Skill Of Effective Signaling In A Negotiation In Order To Get The Best Possible Outcome

- Learn The Skill Of Exploring In A Negotiation: How To Develop The Skill Of Exploring What Is Possible In A Negotiation In Order To Reach The Best Possible Deal

- Learn How To Argue In Your Next Negotiation: How To Develop The Skill Of Effective Arguing In A Negotiation In Order To Get The Best Possible Outcome|

- How To Open Your Next Negotiation: How To Start A Negotiation In Order To Get The Best Possible Outcome

- Preparing For Your Next Negotiation: What You Need To Do BEFORE A Negotiation Starts In Order

To Get The Best Possible Deal

- Learn How To Package Trades In Your Next Negotiation

- All Good Things Come To An End: How To Close A Negotiation - How To Develop The Skill Of Closing In Order To Get The Best Possible Outcome From A Negotiation

- Take No Prisoners In Your Next Negotiation: How To Start A Negotiation In Order To Get The Best Possible Outcome

Miscellaneous

- How To Heal A Broken Leg – Fast!: Understanding how to deal with a broken leg in order to start walking again quickly

- How Software Defined Networking (SDN) Is Going To Change Your World Forever: The Revolution In Network Design And How It Affects You

- The Power Of Virtualization: How It Affects Memory, Servers, and Storage: The Revolution In Creating Virtual Devices And How It Affects You

- The Internet-Enabled Successful School District Superintendent: How To Use The Internet To Boost Parental Involvement In Your Schools

- Power Distribution Unit (PDU) Secrets: What Everyone Who Works In A Data Center Needs To Know!

- Making The Jump: How To Land Your Dream Job When You Get Out Of College!

- How To Use The Internet To Create Successful Students And Involved Parents

"Tips And Techniques That IT Managers Can Use In Order To Develop Leadership Skills"

> This book has been written with one goal in mind – to show you how an IT manager can build needed leadership skills. It's not easy being an IT manager so we're going to show you what you need to be doing in order to not only manage your team, but to also be a leader to them!
>
> **Let's Make Your IT Career A Success!**

What You'll Find Inside:

- **NEW WAYS FOR MANAGERS TO KEEP THE STAFF THAT YOU HAVE**

- **HOW A MANAGER SHOULD PREPARE TO CONDUCT AN INTERVIEW**

- **HOW BIG DATA CAN HELP YOU TO BE A BETTER MANAGER**

- **10 THINGS MANAGERS SHOULD NOT ASK DURING A JOB INTERVIEW**

Dr. Jim Anderson brings his 25 years of real-world experience to this book. He's been an IT manager at some of the world's largest firms. He's going to show you what you need to do (and not do!) in order to successfully manage your career!

www.ingramcontent.com/pod-product-compliance
Lightning Source LLC
Chambersburg PA
CBHW020606220526
45463CB00006B/2472